92
Ful

Radford, Ruby L

73-20

Robert Fulton

DATE DUE

LEX —
RL —
RC —

ROBERT FULTON

About the Book

When Robert Fulton was a boy, he enjoyed drawing pictures and making things. His friends loved his inventions, too — a paddle-wheel boat to fish from and firecrackers for the Fourth of July. Later, when Robert was a man, he painted portraits of famous people and invented a submarine. He built a steamboat, too. People called it Fulton's Folly until they saw how fast it went. Today there are thousands of steamboats all over the world.

A SEE AND READ
BEGINNING TO READ BIOGRAPHY

ROBERT FULTON

by RUBY L. RADFORD

illustrated by
SALEM TAMER

G. P. Putnam's Sons   New York

For Holly Radford

The small boy wrote his name
with his new pencil. ROBERT FULTON.
The lead made good black marks.
Robert smiled. He had made the
pencil himself.

The Fulton family had no money
to buy pencils. Robert's father had
died, and his mother was very poor.
There was money only for food and
clothing — and the children's school.
The Fultons lived in the Pennsylvania
colony in the town of Lancaster.

Robert showed the pencil to his mother.

"I'm proud of you," she said. "Maybe you can mend this pot handle too."

Robert asked the blacksmith to help him. They heated the iron handle in the fire. Then they pounded the parts together on the anvil.

After that Robert mended many things for his mother.

Robert made his own playthings, too. A school friend had given him some paints, but he had no brushes. He made his own with cat's hair and goose quills. An artist gave him free lessons. Soon Robert was painting pictures of his family.

Robert left school after three years
to work for a man who made guns.
Old Peter and his son, Chris, worked
at the gunshop, too.

One day Peter took Robert and
Chris fishing on his old flatboat. They
pushed the boat upstream with poles.
It was hard work. Suddenly Robert
put down his pole.

"There should be an easier way to
take a boat up the creek," he said.

Old Peter laughed. "People have been trying to find easier ways for years. But they can't. A friend of mine, William Henry, tried something once. It didn't work."

"What happened?" asked Robert.

"William Henry put a steam engine on his boat," said Peter. "It was so heavy it broke the boat in two. The boat sank."

"But there *must* be a way to make a boat move faster and more easily," said Robert.

"Yes," said Chris. "Sails are all right for some boats, but not a heavy one like ours."

After that Robert kept trying to think of a better way to move boats.

One day he took some corn to the mill. He watched the paddle wheel turn under the waterfall. The turning wheel made two big stones grind the corn inside the mill.

Maybe a paddle wheel could move a boat, he thought.

14

Robert visited his aunt in the country. He talked about making a boat with a paddle wheel on each side. Then he carved a toy boat like it.

"Maybe someday you can build a big boat like that," his aunt said.

But Robert wanted a better boat
right then. When he went home, his
friends helped him build two big
paddle wheels. They put one on each
side of Peter's old boat. Then Robert
built a crank to turn the wheels.

Robert and his helpers went
aboard the boat. Robert turned the
hand crank. The wheels moved in
the water, and the boat went
forward. The boys let out whoops of
joy! What fun they had fishing in the
paddle-wheel boat!

Soon Robert had little time for play. Most men were going away to fight for freedom from English rule. Many guns were needed. Robert worked long hours at the gunshop.

In the evenings he painted pictures
to sell. He made signs to go over
stores. His mother needed all the
money he could earn for her family
of five.

But July 4, 1777, was a holiday, the first celebration of Independence Day in Lancaster. Robert asked his friends to help him make firecrackers. No one in America had made them before. How surprised people were to see the sparkles lighting up the sky!

When Robert was seventeen, a man from Philadelphia saw some of his paintings.

"I'd like you to paint portraits of all my family," the man said. "You can make more money with your paintings in Philadelphia."

Robert talked with his mother
about it.

"This is a chance you must not
miss," she told him.

She had helped him save some
money. Now they emptied the old
penny jar on the table.

"It is enough for your room and food until you earn more money," she said.

Robert traveled by stagecoach to Philadelphia.

When the portraits were done, he
got more work in a jewelry store.
He painted tiny pictures for ladies'
lockets. Then he painted more
portraits.

Benjamin Franklin was one of the
people who liked them. Franklin was
a printer and inventor.

He told Robert, "Young man, you
should go to England and study
painting."

"I know no one in England, and I haven't much money," said Robert.

Mr. Franklin thought for a moment.

"I shall write to my friend Benjamin West about you. He is now court painter for King George III."

Robert was pleased. "Mr. West lived in Lancaster before I was born," he said. "He painted portraits of both my parents."

"In England he has made many of the royal family. He will teach you more about painting," said Mr. Franklin.

Robert worked hard to save money
for the trip to England. He also
wanted to buy a farm for his mother.

One day he became ill from so much work. The doctor said a sea trip would make him well. But Robert thought of his mother first. He bought her a farm with his money. Then he borrowed more to go to England.

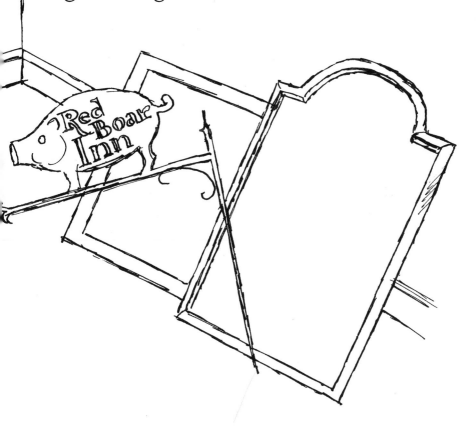

In London he was welcomed by
Mr. and Mrs. West. He lived in their
home while he studied. Soon some of
his pictures were hung in the royal
art gallery. It was a great honor.

Many rich people asked Robert to
paint their portraits. His fortunes had
turned at last. Robert made enough
money to pay his debts. He sent
money to his mother, too.

One day Robert went to the castle of the Duke of Bridgewater to paint a portrait. The duke was a very important man. He owned coal mines and marble quarries. For the first time Robert saw a steam engine pumping water from a coal mine.

He remembered what old Peter
had told him about the heavy steam
engine that had sunk the boat. It
made him want to invent things
again.

The duke had built canals to bring
his coal to market. Robert invented
better ways to work the canals. And
he built a machine to make strong
ropes for the canalboats. Then he
drew pictures of a marble cutter. The
duke had it built in his workshop.

Robert invented many more things
while he was in England. The British
government paid him for some of
them. Robert discovered inventions
paid better than portraits did.

One day Robert thought of a way to help the British Navy. He drew pictures of an underwater boat and a torpedo. He talked to his friends about it.

"A torpedo fired from an underwater boat could destroy pirate ships," he said. "Then the seas would be safe. People could travel to other countries and make friends, instead of fighting."

No one in England would help
Robert build the underwater boat.
The Navy was not even interested.
So Robert decided to go to France.
No one there would help him either.
They called him a dreamer.

Robert had to raise the money to build the boat himself. He painted a large wall picture of Napoleon burning Moscow. Napoleon was then the ruler of France. Crowds of people paid to see the painting.

CONCORD OXBOW SCHOOL

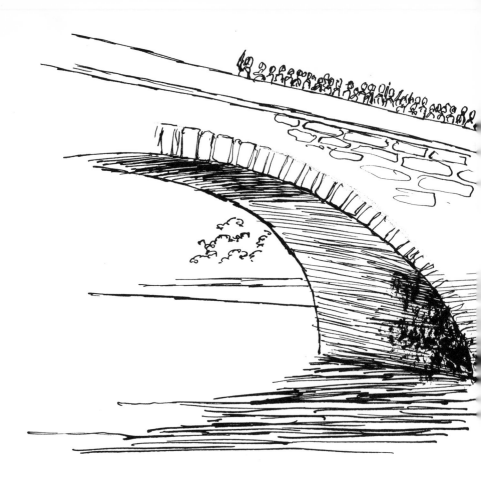

Soon Robert was able to start on
his boat. He hired workmen and
bought wood and iron. After a long
time the underwater boat was put
into the Seine River. Robert named
it the *Nautilus*.

The news spread in Paris that
Robert Fulton was going underwater
in a boat. Crowds gathered on the
riverbank. Many were sure he would
never come up again. Some officers
of the French Navy were watching,
too.

The *Nautilus* was a long, cigar-shaped boat. Robert waved to the people. Then he stepped inside and closed the watertight top. The boat sank into the Seine River. For forty-five minutes the people waited. They began to think they would never see Robert Fulton again.

Then — some distance upstream —
the top of the boat rose slowly out of
the water. Robert stepped out. The
crowds cheered. Robert Fulton had
invented a submarine.

He hoped to sell his idea to the
French Navy. Some officers went
down in the sub with him to fire a
torpedo. The torpedo blew up an old
boat. Robert was sure the Navy
would buy his invention. But
Napoleon was too busy fighting
against England to try anything new.

Robert did not give up. Now he wanted to make a boat move by steam power. He told his idea to Robert Livingston, the American Ambassador to France. He spoke about his underwater boat, too.

"I don't care about a submarine," said the older man. "I want to see your plans for building a steamboat."

Livingston was a rich lawyer. He told Robert, "I believe in you. I've been reading about your work in the newspapers. If you want to form a partnership, I'll put up the money while you do the work."

Robert was very happy. He began work at once on his boat. By the spring of 1803 it was ready to be tried out on the Seine River. A steam engine would turn the paddle wheels.

Just before the trial run a terrible thing happened. A storm blew up in the night. From his room Robert heard a loud crash. He ran to the river to find his boat had sunk.

For the next twenty-four hours he worked to save the boat. He dived many times into the cold water to bring up parts. The next day he was very ill from the hard work in the cold. But after resting in bed, he began to rebuild his boat. This time he made it larger and stronger to hold the heavy engine and boilers.

On August 8, 1805, he filled the
furnace with logs and heated the
boiler. Smoke rose from the tall
smokestack. Soon the boat began to
move, but Robert could not make it
go faster than four miles an hour. He

showed the watchers onshore how
the boat could turn around and
come back. His boat was a success!
At last he had done what he had
planned when he was a boy. He had
made a steamboat that would really
run.

The French newspapers called
Fulton a genius. But Robert wanted
to make a better boat. He decided to
build it in America.

Robert had been away for twenty
years. He was happy to be home and
to be at work on a new boat.

Livingston got permission for them
to try a steamboat on the Hudson
River.

Before long Robert's new boat was
finished. Many people called it
Fulton's Folly. They did not believe
it would ever run.

Robert named his boat the
Clermont. He invited some friends to
make the first trip with him. Among
them was Harriet Livingston, his
partner's pretty niece. Robert was
already in love with her. If his boat
were a success, he would have
money enough to get married.

On August 9, 1807, the *Clermont* started up the Hudson. The whistle blew. They were off! Some people on the dock cheered. Others jeered. They were sure the boat would sink. Then suddenly it did stop!

Robert yelled to the crowd, "Wait! I'll find the trouble!"

Soon he and the engineer fixed
what was wrong. Then they started
off again. All the way up the Hudson
people waved and cheered. They
had never seen such a sight!

Thirty-two hours later they reached
Albany. It was 150 miles from New
York. The new boat was much faster
than the first.

After that Fulton and Livingston built many more steamboats. Soon some were running on the Mississippi River. They helped farmers and lumbermen ship their goods up and down the great rivers. More people moved west. And the country grew richer because of Robert Fulton's invention.

Not long after his first trip up the Hudson Robert married Harriet Livingston. They had three daughters and one son. Robert was then a very rich and happy man. His children loved to hear about the first paddle-wheel boat, turned with a crank.

"But I think you were the bravest
man in the world when you went
down in your submarine," said his
young son.

Robert always remembered the
struggles and dangers of building his
boats. But he knew the world was a
better place because he had kept on
trying.

After Robert Fulton died, a bronze
bust of him was placed in the Hall
of Fame in New York City. But the
greatest memorials to Fulton are the
thousands of steamboats on rivers
and seas around the world.

KEY WORDS

anvil
blacksmith
boiler
canal
crank
engine
firecracker
gallery

government
handle
invent
jewelry
lead
marble
memorial
paddle

partnership
portrait
quarries
quill
stagecoach
steam
submarine
torpedo

The Author

Ruby L. Radford is the author of more than fifty books for children and young adults. She has also written for magazines and for radio and television. A resident of Augusta, Georgia, Miss Radford was named "Georgia's Author of the Year" in 1969.

The Artist

Salem Tamer studied art at Vesper George School in Boston and the Art Students League of New York. He has won several prizes for his book and magazine illustration, advertising art, book jackets, and industrial publications.

CONCORD OXBOW SCHOOL